Seals, Sea Lions, Walruses

Kids Animated Book

Billy Grinslott & Kinsey Marie Books

ISBN - 9781965098318

The Mediterranean monk seal is one of the rarest marine mammals in the world. There are only about 700 Mediterranean Monk seals. They are found around the Mediterranean Sea and the Northwest African Coast. They are earless seals. They can't hear good on land but have great hearing in the water. Mediterranean monk seals swim so fast and agile that they can outmaneuver a shark.

Hawaiian monk seals live around the Hawaiian Islands and Johnston Atoll. They shed their top layer of fur every year. They can dive more than 1,800 feet and remain under water for up to 20 minutes. They like to sleep on beaches for days at a time. All Monk seals prefer warm tropical water, not cold water like other seals. They can't rotate their hind flippers underneath their bodies, like other seals.

Ross Seals have a smaller, wider head, with a short snout. They also have a small mouth and the shortest hair of any seal. Ross Seals live in the Southern Ocean waters surrounding Antarctica and some sub-Antarctic islands. Ross seals are known to make distinctive warbling and trilling calls. They can dive up to 2500 feet and stay under water for up to 30 minutes.

Elephant seals get their name because their nose is like an elephant's trunk. Male elephant seals weigh as much as a small truck or cargo van. Elephant seals spend up to 80% of their lives in the ocean. They can hold their breath for more than 100 minutes when swimming. They can swim 60 miles a day. Elephant seals live for just two months of the year on land. They are the largest seal in the world.

Leopard seals got their name because they have spots like a leopard. Leopard seals are the third largest seal in the world. Sometimes leopard seal's smile. Leopard seals sing underwater. They have been known to give fish to humans. Leopard seals sometimes play with their food like kids do. Leopard seals can hold their breath for about 15 minutes while swimming.

Crabeater seals do not actually eat crabs. Crabeater Seals have a unique adaptation for feeding. They have evolved a sieve-like tooth structure that filter krill. They suck in water containing krill, close their jaws, and then force the water back out between their specialized teeth, trapping the krill inside.

Hooded seals live in the cold waters of the North Atlantic and Arctic Oceans. Adult males are known for the stretchy cavity, or hood, in their nose, which they can inflate so that it looks like a bright red balloon. Hooded seals are also known as bladder-nosed seals. Hooded seals are about 8.5 feet long and weigh about 750 pounds. They have silver-gray fur with darker patches of different sizes and shapes across their bodies.

Weddell Seals live the furthest south of any mammals. Weddell Seals are the most studied of any Seal species in the Antarctic. Females are a little bit bigger than males. They live around Antarctica in the Southern Ocean. They keep breathing holes in the ice open by rasping back and forth with their teeth, this allows them to live in ice covered areas. They have large eyes that help them to search for food in the sea where light is limited under the ice. Weddell seals are impressive divers, they can dive 1900 feet and be underwater for 80 minutes.

There are 5 different types of Harbor seals. They have a wide range of color variations. Harbor seals rarely interact with one another. Seals swim with an alternate back-and-forth movement with their hind flippers. They can stay under water for 30 minutes. Harbor seals are curious but shy, they prefer quiet areas. They are one of the most common seals. They have the largest geographical range of any seal. Harbor seals can swim in fresh or saltwater.

The Bearded Seal got its name because of its long whiskers that looks like a beard. Bearded seals are the largest seal species in the Arctic, reaching a maximum length of 8 feet and weight of 950 pounds. Bearded seal pups can swim and dive up to 6560 feet within hours of being born. Bearded seals are very vocal and create trill sounds that can be heard up to 12 miles away. Bearded seals can sleep vertically in the ocean with their heads just above the surface.

Spotted Seals have a small body, a rounded head, and short flippers. The coats of adults have dark spots over light gray to silver. Spotted seals are relatively shy and are difficult to approach. The largest groups of spotted seals can be found in Alaska. Spotted seals dive to depths up to 1,000 feet. They can swim underwater for 30 minutes or longer, without coming up for air. Spotted seal pups are born with a white, fluffy coat of fur.

Ringed Seals get their name from the circular rings on their fur coat. Ringed seals can live in areas that are completely covered with ice. They use their sharp claws to make and maintain their own breathing holes through the ice. The ringed seal is the smallest of all living seal species. It lives on the Arctic Sea ice and ocean. Female ringed seals create lairs for their pups in the sea ice surface, which provide protection from extreme weather and predators.

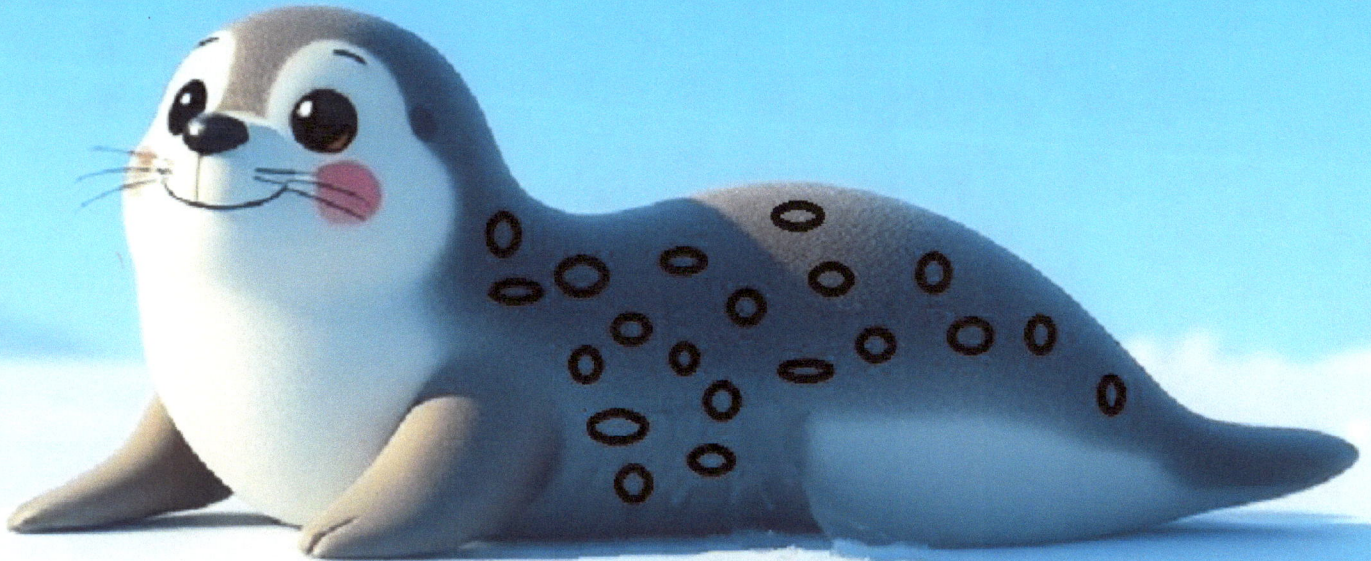

The Caspian seal is one of the smallest members of the earless seal family. Caspian seals, are the only marine mammal that live in the Caspian Sea . Caspian seals tend to live in large groups. Caspian seals are shallow divers, they don't like deep water. Caspian seal pups cannot enter the water until they molt and get their adult fur, because their pup fur is not insulated and if they get wet they will freeze.

Baikal seals, live in Lake Baikal in Siberia, they are found nowhere else in the world. Baikal seals can dive as deep as 1300 feet. They can stay underwater for up to 70 minutes. They have large eyes to see better at deeper depths and they use their whiskers to locate food. Baikal seals are the smallest species of seal in the world. They are covered with silvery grey fur. Baikal seals can give birth to twins, one of the few seal species to do so.

The ribbon seal has a distinctive coat pattern of light-colored bands or ribbons on a dark background. Ribbon seals live in the North Pacific Ocean and Arctic Ocean. Ribbon seals spend most of their time in the open ocean and on pack ice. Ribbon seal adults are about 5 to 6 feet long and weigh about 200 to 330 pounds. Ribbon seals move across the ice in a caterpillar-like movement. They alternate fore flipper strokes to pull themselves forward while moving their head and hips in a side-to-side motion.

Harp seal pups are born with white fur that helps them stay warm. Pups shed their white fur after about four weeks. Harp seals can stay underwater for at least 16 minutes at a time. Harp seals are named for the curved, black patch on their backs, which resembles a harp. Harp seal pups call to their mothers by bawling. They have over 19 different calls. Harp seals prefer to remain in the water swimming. They can dive to depths of 1300 feet. Harp seals are sociable animals that enjoy the company of other seals.

South American Fur Seals are dark brown or gray in color. When mature they develop longer fur around their shoulders and necks. They are social animals and live alongside each other in rocks that are along the shore. These seals often fish during the night in groups. They live in the Pacific and Atlantic coasts of South America. These seals are very playful and get the nickname dogs of the sea because of their playfulness like dogs.

Subantarctic Fur Seals can be found in the South Atlantic and Indian oceans, they live on islands near Gough, Amsterdam, and Prince Edward Islands. They are known to migrate over 300 miles away to forage for food. Subantarctic fur seals look like they have a face mask, with a dark brown body and cream-colored fur around their faces and necks.

The brown fur seal belongs to a large seal species from Australia and South Africa. Brown fur seals are diurnal, being active during the daytime and sleeping at night. They like to share the same area every year, they live in groups called colonies. The brown fur seal is the largest member of the fur seal family. They have external ear flaps, unlike many seals. Brown fur seals are common, there's over 2 million worldwide. While foraging, the brown fur seal can dive up to 270 feet.

Antarctic fur seals are mostly distributed in Subantarctic islands. Adult males are dark brown, females and juveniles are gray. Pups are black when born and turn to a silver-gray color when they are 2 to 3 months old. Antarctic fur seals nearly became extinct during the time of the 18th and 19th centuries. Now the Antarctic fur seals are the most abundant species of fur seal. There's an estimated population of 4 million seals.

The gray seal is found on both shores of the North Atlantic Ocean. Gray Seals spend most of their time out at sea feeding on fish. Gray seals give birth to fluffy white pups. The pups stay on land until they have lost their white coats. Gray seals typically dive in shallow waters but have been recorded diving down to 1,300 feet. Gray seals dive underwater for a maximum time of 30 minutes. Gray seals can spend more than two days out at sea.

Galapagos fur seals are typically found on the rocky shores of the western islands of the Galapagos Archipelago. Galápagos Fur Seals are smaller than sea lions, but their front flippers are larger. Their coat is dense and luxuriant, consisting of two layers of hair that vary from brown to gray. Females remain with their newborn pups for a week before leaving to feed. Galapagos fur seals have large eyes so that they can swim at night. They are the smallest of all seals.

The Juan Fernández fur seal is the second smallest of the fur seals. They are found only on the Pacific Coast of South America, more specifically on the Juan Fernández Islands and other islands off the coast of Chile. Mothers will stay with their pups for 11 days after having a pup, this is longer than any other fur seals.

The Guadalupe fur seal was nearly extinct in the 1880's with a known population numbering only 7 individuals left in 1892. Mothers and pups of all seals identify each other by unique vocalizations, noises, and scent. Guadalupe fur seals are found in coastal rocky habitats and caves in the tropical waters of California and Mexico. Guadalupe fur seals grow to a maximum length of 7 feet and weight of 400 pounds.

New Zealand Fur Seals have a pointy nose, unlike other seals. Their coat is dark grey to brown. When wet, they look almost black. They live in New Zealand and in some parts of Australia. They can dive deeper and longer than any other species of fur seal. When seals lift their front and hind flippers out of the water, this is a behavior known as jugging. They do this to dry off and stay warm by shedding or shaking off cold water. Kind of like a dog when they shake to remove water.

Northern fur seals are known for their thick brown fur, which gives them their name. There are about 300,000 hairs on each square inch of their bodies. Adult northern fur seals spend more than 300 days per year at sea. Adult males grow short, bushy manes with lighter-colored fur around their neck and shoulders. Northern fur seals inhabit the Northern Pacific Ocean from southern California to Japan and as far as the Bering Sea.

Australian sea lions are found along the southern and western coastlines of Australia. They're also one of the rarest seals in the world. While male Australian sea lions travel long distances, females will rarely ever move from where they were born. They are homebodies and like to stay in one area. They are highly sociable and gather in large colonies on land.

California sea lions are known for their intelligence, playfulness, and noisy barking or bawling. Their piercing barking can be heard from a quite a distance. Their fur color ranges from brown seen in males to a lighter, golden light brown seen in females. California sea lions are found from Vancouver Island in British Columbia to the southern tip of Baja California in Mexico. They also live on the Galápagos Islands.

Galapagos sea lions are found in two places, the Galapagos Islands and on Isla de la Plata, which is about 25 miles off the coast of Ecuador. They are one of only a few marine mammals that live in the Galapagos. They stay relatively close to shore and don't like venturing out to sea much. Galapagos sea lions are not afraid of people. Young Galapagos sea lions love to swim with people.

Japanese Sea Lions were considered a relative or subspecies of the California sea lion. In the 1970's the Japanese sea lion went extinct. Due to overfishing and damage to their habitat and feeding areas, the Japanese sea lion became extinct in the 1970's. There are other seals and seal lions species that could face extinction, like the Japanese sea lion, if we don't help protect them.

New Zealand sea lions are one of the rarest sea lion species in the world and are only found in New Zealand. New Zealand Sea Lion is one of the largest animals found in New Zealand. The New Zealand sea lion numbers around 12,000 and is one of the world's rarest sea lion species.

South American Sea Lions can be found along the coasts and offshore islands of South America from Zorritos in northern Peru to Ilha dos Lobos in southern Brazil. On land sea lions will use their rear flippers to walk, climb and gallop, and can move surprisingly fast. Sea lions sleep both during the day and the night and are able to sleep either in or out of water. Adult males have a large head and mane like a lion.

Steller sea lions can be found along the North Pacific Ocean. Adult males may be up to 11 feet long and can weigh up to 2,500 pounds. Adult females are 7.5 to 9.5 feet long and weigh up to 800 pounds. Adult males are further distinguished by long, coarse hair on the chest, shoulders, and back. Steller sea lions are the world's largest species of sea lions. Steller sea lions are golden brown in color.

There are only 2 types of walruses, the Atlantic and Pacific. Both male and female walruses have long tusks. Mother walruses are very protective of their young. A walrus can live to be 40 years old. Walruses don't like swimming in deep water. Walruses rest on ice or on shore. Thick layers of blubber protect walruses from the cold arctic temperatures. Walruses weigh up to 1.5 tons, as much as some cars. Walruses can sleep in water. They are very sociable and like to hang out with their friends.

Fun Facts About Seals & Sea Lions

Seals use bawling, clicking or trilling noises to communicate.

Their calls are referred to as barks like a dog.

They have blubber to keep them warm in cold water.

The biggest seal can weigh more than 8,000 pounds.

The largest seals can be 21 feet long.

Seals live on average for 20-30 years.

Seals eat fish, birds, and shellfish.

Male seals are called bulls.

Females are called cows.

Baby Seals are called pups.

Seals and Sea Lions can learn tricks.

Fun Facts About Seals & Sea Lions

Some seals can dive to really deep depths.

Some seals can stay underwater up to 80 minutes.

Seals can sleep in the water as well as on land.

They can see both above and under the water.

Sea Lions are not able to smell under water.

On land they use their rear flippers to walk.

Sea lions produce loud roars like lions do.

Some sea lions have manes like lions do.

On land, they breathe through their nostrils.

Their nostrils shut when they dive underwater.

What's the difference between seals and sea lions?

Seals, sea lions and walruses, are pinnipeds, which means, fin footed in Latin.

Sea lions walk on land using their large flippers. Seals have small flippers, wriggle on their bellies on land or ice.

Sea lions have small flaps for outer ears. Earless or true seals lack external ears altogether. They have tiny holes on the sides of their head for ear canals.

Sea lions bark loudly and are noisy. Seals are quieter, vocalizing via soft grunts and other chattering noises.

Sea lions prefer to be on land. Seals are more aquadynamic than sea lions and love being in the water. Seals hind flippers angle backward and don't rotate underneath like see lions. This makes them fast in the water but basic belly crawlers on ice or land.

Sea lions can walk on land by rotating their hind flippers forward and underneath their bodies. This is why they are more likely to be seen in shows.

Author Page

Billy Grinslott & Kinsey Marie Books

ISBN – 9781965098318

Thanks

www.ingramcontent.com/pod-product-compliance
Lightning Source LLC
Chambersburg PA
CBHW060833270326
41933CB00002B/78